BARBECUE

TRADITIONAL AND MODERN RECIPES
FOR A SUMMER BARBECUE

LINDA DOESER

MAIN PHOTOGRAPHY BY IAN PARSONS

This is a Parragon Book
This edition published in 2006

Parragon
Queen Street House
4 Queen Street
Bath BA1 1HE, UK

Created and produced for Parragon by The Bridgewater Book Company Ltd.

Cover by Talking Design

Home economists Sara Hesketh and Richard Green
Additional photography Calvey Taylor-Haw (10, 34, 46, 54, 94)

ISBN: 1-40547-733-4

Printed in China

NOTE

*This book uses metric and imperial measurements. Follow the same units of
measurement throughout; do not mix metric and imperial. All spoon measurements
are level: teaspoons are assumed to be 5 ml and tablespoons are assumed to be 15 ml.
Unless otherwise stated, milk is assumed to be full fat, eggs and individual vegetables
such as potatoes are medium, and pepper is freshly ground black pepper.*

*The times given for each recipe are an approximate guide only. The preparation times may
differ according to the techniques used by different people and the cooking times may vary
as a result of the type of oven used. Ovens should be preheated to the specified temperature.
If using a fan-assisted oven, check the manufacturer's instructions for adjusting the time and
temperature. The preparation times include chilling and marinating times, where appropriate.*

*Recipes using raw or very lightly cooked eggs should be avoided by infants, the elderly,
pregnant women, convalescents and anyone suffering from an illness.*

Contents

Introduction

Cooking food outdoors on a barbecue is great fun and a delicious way of feeding a crowd. To keep everybody happy, it is always a good idea to offer a range of meat and seafood dishes, vegetables, salads and desserts, so there is something for meat-eaters, vegetarians and even fussy children.

The dishes can be as straightforward or complicated as you wish. You can start by elaborate dishes. Thread seafood, poultry, vegetables or fruit on to wooden skewers to make kebabs. Add extra flavour and succulence to the food by mixing various marinades and dressings.

The key to a successful barbecue is good planning. It helps to know roughly how many people are coming. If the numbers are very vague or large, you need to lay on a plentiful supply of

basics, such as burgers, salad and bread, so that nobody goes hungry. Reserve supplies can be kept in the refrigerator and frozen later if not needed.

cooking a basic barbecue with traditional ingredients such as sausages, burgers, chicken drumsticks, chops and steaks. Served with burger buns, French bread or baked potatoes and plenty of fresh leafy or mixed salad, good food doesn't get much easier.

Once you have got the hang of cooking on your barbecue, you can experiment with more

To cater for vegetarian guests, prepare plenty of vegetable kebabs and parcels which others can eat too. Offer different fillings to go with baked potatoes: a creamy cheese or a spicy sweetcorn relish are very popular. A good selection of colourful salads, including a pasta, rice, tomato or mixed bean salad, will please vegetarians and appeal to everyone else as well.

Safety

Barbecuing is a safe way of cooking as long as you take a few sensible precautions.

• Position your barbecue away from overhanging trees and shrubs to avoid branches catching fire. Have a bucket of water nearby in case the fire blows out of control.

• Trim off excess fat and shake away surplus

marinade before putting the food on the barbecue to stop fat dripping down on to the hot coals and bursting into flames.

• To minimize the risk of food poisoning, make sure that meat and seafood are cooked through. Test the meat by piercing it with a skewer or the tip of a sharp knife – it is cooked when the juices run clear (not pink). Once it has cooled down, never return poultry to the grill to finish cooking.

• Keep salads and cooked foods away from raw meat. Use different chopping boards, utensils,

tea towels and plates for dealing with raw and cooked meats or salad ingredients.

• On hot days, store foods out of direct sunlight and keep them chilled for as long as possible before cooking or serving. Cover food with netting or clean tea towels to keep insects off.

• Never leave the barbecue unattended. Warn any small children to keep away from the hot fire. Ban pets from the food and cooking areas as well, to prevent contamination and accidents.

• Use long-handled utensils and oven gloves to avoid getting burned and splashed.

• The person cooking should go easy on the alcohol, as a drunken cook can be a dangerous one. Discourage other adults who have been drinking from cooking too.

Equipment

There are many different types of fuel, and an equally wide range of barbecues, so you should consider your exact requirements before spending any money.

Types of fuel

First, decide on the fuel you want to use:

- Lumpwood charcoal is readily available, inexpensive and easy to light, but burns quickly.
- Charcoal briquettes take longer to catch, but burn for a long time and produce little smoke.
- Self-igniting charcoal is lumpwood charcoal or charcoal briquettes that have been coated with a flammable chemical. They light easily but you cannot start cooking until the chemical has burnt off as it can taint the food.
- Wood fires need constant attention. Hardwoods, such as oak and apple, are best as they burn slowly and have a pleasant smell. Softwoods burn too fast and tend to spark.
- Wood chips and herbs, such as sprigs of thyme or rosemary, can be sprinkled on the fire to give off a delicious aroma.

Choosing your barbecue

Before buying a barbecue, consider the number of people you will want to feed; how often you are likely to use it; how it will fit into your garden, and how much you are prepared to spend on it.

- Disposable barbecues are inexpensive foil trays with enough fuel to burn for about one hour – ideal for a small, one-off picnic.
- Hibachi or 'firebox' barbecues from Japan are small, lightweight, reusable and easy to transport.
- Portable barbecues are light and easy to fold up and carry in the boot of a car for larger picnics.
- Brazier barbecues can be moved about the garden and stored easily. Some are a little low so check that the one you are thinking of buying is a comfortable height for the person who will be doing most of the cooking. If your garden is windy, choose one with a hood to protect the open grill.
- Kettle-grill barbecues are the next best thing to a permanent barbecue. The lid covers the grill and can save a barbecue party if it starts to rain. Many have a spit-roast for cooking chickens and joints.
- Gas and electric barbecues are expensive but easy to operate and very quick – they only take ten minutes to warm up. However, they do not give the food the traditional smoky flavour it gets from being cooked over charcoal.
- Permanent, tailor-made barbecues are an excellent choice if you barbecue frequently. You can buy kits or use simple materials such as house bricks and firebricks to build a fireplace and fit an adjustable metal rack.

Preparation

is possible to make some dishes for your
rbecue, such as burgers and meat kebabs, well
advance and freeze them. Then all you have to
 is remember to take them out the night before
d thaw them thoroughly before cooking.
ternatively, you can make them the previous
y and store them in the refrigerator overnight.
u may also start marinating food the day before.

   Leave the chopping and mixing of any salad
gredients until the morning of the barbecue.
ss in the dressing just before you are ready
 serve them, so that the leaves and other
gredients do not go limp and soggy.

Hints and tips

• Remember to light your barbecue at least an
hour before you want to start cooking, to make
sure it will be hot. For setting the fire, follow the
instructions that come with the fuel you are using.

• To ensure even and thorough cooking, do not
place too much food on the grill rack at once.

• To avoid contamination, aim to cook the same
types of food together. Do not mix meat, fish and
vegetarian dishes on the grill. The best plan is to
wrap the vegetarian ingredients in foil parcels.

• Foil-wrapped potatoes work well, especially
if you bake them in a conventional oven at
200°C/400°F/Gas Mark 6 for 30 minutes before
moving them to the barbecue to finish cooking.

• Foil parcels are often the best solution for hot
desserts. Just wrap the fruit and leave it to
cook around the edge of the grill where the
temperature is slightly lower.

• Offer a choice of drinks, both alcoholic and non-
alcoholic: a fruit punch is usually popular.

• Even when rain stops play, you can keep cooking
if you shut the lid of your barbecue and open the
vents. Alternatively, you can take the food inside
and carry on cooking under the grill in your
kitchen. When the sun comes out again you can
move back into the garden.

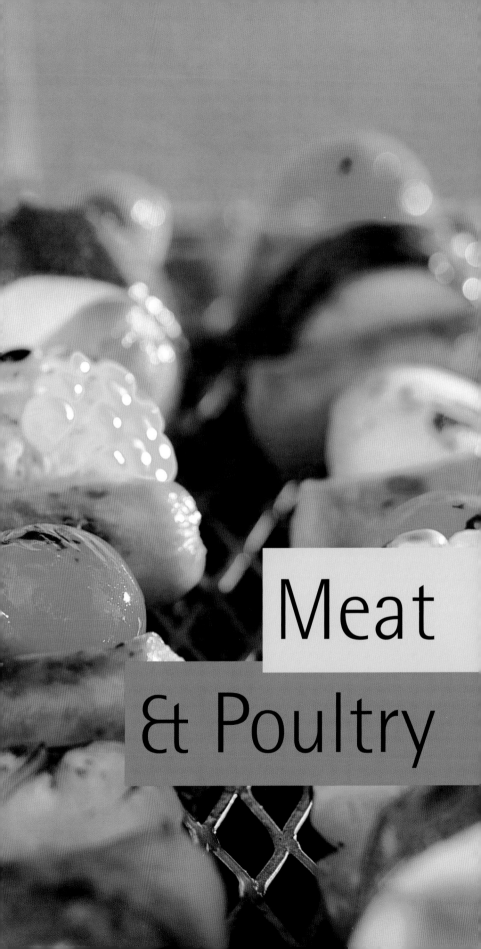

Meat & Poultry

Tabasco Steaks with Watercress Butter

A variation on a classic theme, this simple but rather extravagant dish would be ideal for a special occasion barbecue party.

serves 4

1 bunch of watercress

85 g/3 oz unsalted butter, softened

4 sirloin steaks, about 225 g/8 oz each

4 tsp Tabasco sauce

salt and pepper

Method

❶ Preheat the barbecue. Using a sharp knife, finely chop enough watercress to fill 4 tablespoons. Reserve a few watercress leaves for the garnish. Place the butter in a small bowl and beat in the chopped watercress with a fork until fully incorporated. Cover with clingfilm and leave to chill in the refrigerator until required.

❷ Sprinkle each steak with 1 teaspoon of the Tabasco sauce, rubbing it in well. Season to taste with salt and pepper.

❸ Cook the steaks over hot coals, 2½ minutes each side for rare, 4 minutes each side for medium and 6 minutes each side for well done. Transfer to serving plates, garnish with the reserved watercress leaves and serve immediately, topped with the watercress butter.

Variation

If you like, substitute the same amount of fresh parsley for the watercress.

Best Ever Burgers

Barbecues and burgers are almost inseparable. However, these succulent, home-made burgers bear no resemblance to the little ready-made patties available in most shops.

serves 6

900 g/2 lb lean minced steak
2 onions, finely chopped
25 g/1 oz fresh white breadcrumbs
1 egg, lightly beaten
1½ tsp finely chopped
fresh thyme
salt and pepper

To serve
6 sesame seed baps
2 tomatoes
1 onion
lettuce leaves
mayonnaise
mustard
tomato ketchup

Method

❶ Preheat the barbecue. Place the steak, onions, breadcrumbs, egg and thyme in a large glass bowl and season to taste with salt and pepper. Mix thoroughly using your hands.

❷ Form the mixture into 6 large patties with your hands, neatening the edges with a round-bladed knife.

❸ Cook the burgers over hot coals for 3–4 minutes on each side. Meanwhile, cut the baps in half and briefly toast on the barbecue, cut-side down. Using a sharp knife, slice the tomatoes and cut the onion into thinly sliced rings. Fill the toasted baps with the cooked burgers, lettuce, sliced tomatoes and onion rings and serve immediately, with the mayonnaise, mustard and tomato ketchup.

Variation

For Tex-Mex burgers, add 2 deseeded and finely chopped fresh green chillies to the mixture in Step 1 and serve with guacamole.

Luxury Cheeseburgers

This is a sophisticated version of the traditional burger with a surprise filling of melted blue cheese. Serve with plenty of salad leaves to make a substantial barbecue lunch.

serves 4

55 g/2 oz Stilton cheese
450 g/1 lb lean minced steak
1 onion, finely chopped
1 celery stick, finely chopped
1 tsp creamed horseradish
1 tbsp chopped fresh thyme
salt and pepper

To serve
4 sesame seed baps
lettuce leaves
sliced tomatoes

Method

❶ Preheat the barbecue. Crumble the Stilton cheese into a bowl and reserve until required. Place the steak, onion, celery, horseradish and thyme in a separate bowl and season to taste with salt and pepper. Mix thoroughly using your hands.

❷ Form the mixture into 8 patties with your hands and a round-bladed knife. Divide the cheese between 4 of them and top with the remaining patties. Gently press them together and mould the edges.

❸ Cook the burgers over hot coals for 5 minutes on each side. Meanwhile, cut the baps in half and briefly toast on the barbecue, cut-side down. Fill the baps with the cooked burgers, lettuce and tomato slices and serve immediately.

Variation

Substitute Wensleydale or Lancashire cheese for the Stilton cheese and finely snipped chives for the thyme.

Rack & Ruin

This quick and easy dish is perfect for serving as part of a summer party menu, along with plenty of salad and potatoes.

serves 4

4 racks of lamb, each with 4 cutlets

2 tbsp extra virgin olive oil

1 tbsp balsamic vinegar

1 tbsp lemon juice

3 tbsp finely chopped fresh rosemary

1 small onion, finely chopped

salt and pepper

Method

❶ Place the racks of lamb in a large, shallow, non-metallic dish. Make a marinade by placing the oil, vinegar, lemon juice, rosemary and onion in a jug and stirring together. Season to taste with salt and pepper.

❷ Pour the marinade over the lamb and turn until thoroughly coated. Cover with clingfilm and marinate in the refrigerator for 1 hour, turning occasionally.

❸ Preheat the barbecue. Drain the racks of lamb, reserving the marinade. Cook over medium-hot coals, brushing frequently with the marinade, for 10 minutes on each side. Serve immediately.

Minted Lamb Steaks

You can prepare this dish with any kind of lamb chops – leg chops are especially tender – or cutlets, in which case you will probably require two per serving. Shoulder steaks also work well.

serves 6

6 chump chops, about 175 g/6 oz each

150 ml/5 fl oz natural Greek yogurt

2 garlic cloves, finely chopped

1 tsp grated fresh root ginger

1/4 tsp coriander seeds, crushed

salt and pepper

1 tbsp olive oil, plus extra for brushing

1 tbsp orange juice

1 tsp walnut oil

2 tbsp chopped fresh mint

Method

❶ Place the chops in a large, shallow, non-metallic bowl. Mix half the yogurt, the garlic, ginger and coriander seeds together in a jug and season to taste with salt and pepper. Spoon the mixture over the chops, turning to coat them evenly, then cover with clingfilm and leave to marinate in the refrigerator for 2 hours, turning occasionally.

❷ Preheat the barbecue. Place the remaining yogurt, the olive oil, orange juice, walnut oil and mint in a small bowl and, using a hand-held whisk, whisk until thoroughly blended. Season to taste with salt and pepper. Cover the minted yogurt with clingfilm and leave to chill in the refrigerator until ready to serve.

❸ Drain the chops, scraping off the marinade. Brush with olive oil and cook over medium-hot coals for 5–7 minutes on each side. Serve immediately with the minted yogurt.

Variation

If you like, omit the orange juice and walnut oil and stir in 1/4 teaspoon ground star anise and a pinch each of ground cinnamon and ground cumin.

Normandy Brochettes

The orchards of Normandy are famous throughout France, providing both eating apples and cider-making varieties. For an authentic touch, enjoy a glass of Calvados between courses.

serves 4

450 g/1 lb pork fillet

300 ml/10 fl oz dry cider

1 tbsp finely chopped fresh sage

6 black peppercorns, crushed

2 crisp eating apples

1 tbsp sunflower oil

Method

❶ Using a sharp knife, cut the pork into 2.5-cm/1-inch cubes, then place in a large, shallow, non-metallic dish. Mix the cider, sage and peppercorns together in a jug, pour the mixture over the pork and turn until thoroughly coated. Cover with clingfilm and leave to marinate in the refrigerator for 1–2 hours.

❷ Preheat the barbecue. Drain the pork, reserving the marinade. Core the apples, but do not peel, then cut into wedges. Dip the apple wedges into the reserved marinade and thread on to several metal skewers, alternating with the cubes of pork. Stir the sunflower oil into the remaining marinade.

❸ Cook the brochettes over medium-hot coals, turning and brushing frequently with the reserved marinade, for 12–15 minutes. Transfer to a large serving plate and, if you prefer, remove the meat and apples from the skewers before serving. Serve immediately.

Variation

Replace 1 apple with 6 no-soak dried prunes wrapped in strips of streaky bacon. Thread the prunes on to the skewers with the remaining apple and pork.

Sausages with Barbecue Sauce

Although there is much more to barbecues than sausages, they can make a welcome appearance from time to time. This delicious sauce is a wonderful excuse for including them.

serves 4

2 tbsp sunflower oil

1 large onion, chopped

2 cloves garlic, chopped

225 g/8 oz canned chopped tomatoes

1 tbsp Worcestershire sauce

2 tbsp brown fruity sauce

2 tbsp light muscovado sugar

4 tbsp white wine vinegar

½ tsp mild chilli powder

¼ tsp mustard powder

dash of Tabasco sauce

450 g/1 lb sausages

salt and pepper

bread finger rolls, to serve

Method

❶ To make the sauce, heat the oil in a small saucepan and fry the onion and garlic for 4–5 minutes until softened and just beginning to brown.

❷ Add the tomatoes, Worcestershire sauce, brown fruity sauce, sugar, white wine vinegar, chilli powder, mustard powder and Tabasco sauce to the saucepan. Add salt and pepper to taste, and bring to the boil.

❸ Reduce the heat and simmer gently for 10–15 minutes until the sauce begins to thicken slightly. Stir occasionally so that the sauce does not burn and stick to the bottom of the saucepan. Set aside and keep warm until required.

❹ Preheat the barbecue. Cook the sausages over hot coals for 10–15 minutes, turning frequently. Do not prick them with a fork or the juices and fat will run out and cause the barbecue to flare.

❺ Insert the sausages into the bread rolls and serve with the barbecue sauce.

Variation

Choose any tasty sausages for this recipe. Lincolnshire sausages are a good choice as are Cumberland sausages, which are also available in a coil (secure the coil with skewers so that it does not unravel as it cooks). Venison sausages have a gamey flavour and taste wonderful cooked on the barbecue.

Meatballs on Sticks

These are popular with children and adults alike. Serve with a selection of
ready-made or home-made sauces, such as a tomato relish,
heated on the side of the barbecue.

serves 8

4 pork and herb sausages

115 g/4 oz fresh beef mince

85 g/3 oz fresh white breadcrumbs

1 onion, finely chopped

2 tbsp chopped mixed fresh herbs, such as
parsley, thyme and sage

1 egg

salt and pepper

sunflower oil, for brushing

sauces of your choice, to serve

Method

❶ Preheat the barbecue. Remove the sausage meat from the skins, place in a large bowl and break up with a fork. Add the beef mince, breadcrumbs, onion, herbs and egg. Season to taste with salt and pepper and stir well with a wooden spoon until thoroughly mixed.

❷ Form the mixture into small balls, about the size of a golf ball, between the palms of your hands. Spear each one with a cocktail stick and brush with oil.

❸ Cook over medium-hot coals, turning frequently and brushing with more oil as necessary, for 10 minutes, or until cooked through. Transfer to a large serving plate and serve immediately with a choice of warmed sauces.

Variation

Substitute 1 cooked potato and 1 cooked small beetroot, both finely chopped, for the breadcrumbs.

Bacon Koftas

Koftas – moulded kebabs – are usually made from a spicy mixture of minced lamb. These ones are economically based on lean bacon. While they are very easy to make, be careful not to over-process them.

serves 4

1 small onion

225 g/8 oz lean bacon, rinded and roughly chopped

85 g/3 oz fresh white breadcrumbs

1 tbsp chopped fresh marjoram

grated rind of 1 lemon

1 egg white

pepper

chopped nuts, for coating (optional)

paprika, to dust

snipped fresh chives, to garnish

Method

❶ Preheat the barbecue. Using a sharp knife, chop the onion, then put it into a food processor with the bacon, breadcrumbs, marjoram, lemon rind and egg white. Season to taste with pepper and process briefly, just until the mixture is blended.

❷ Divide the bacon mixture into 8 equal portions and form each around a skewer into a fat sausage. Dust the skewered koftas with paprika. If you like, form 4 of the portions into rounds rather than sausages, then spread the chopped nuts out on a large, flat plate and roll the rounds in them to coat.

❸ Cook over hot coals for 10 minutes, turning frequently. Transfer to a large serving plate and serve immediately, garnished with snipped fresh chives.

Fabulous Frankfurter Skewers

A new way with an old favourite – cook frankfurter sausages on the barbecue for a wonderful smoky flavour and an incredibly easy meal. They are served here with garlic toast.

serves 4

12 frankfurter sausages

2 courgettes, cut into 1-cm/½-inch slices

2 corn cobs, cut into 1-cm/½-inch slices

12 cherry tomatoes

12 baby onions

2 tbsp olive oil

Garlic toast

2 garlic bulbs

2–3 tbsp olive oil

1 baguette, sliced

salt and pepper

Method

❶ Preheat the barbecue. To make the garlic toast, slice off the tops of the garlic bulbs. Brush the bulbs with oil and wrap them in foil. Cook over hot coals, turning occasionally, for 30 minutes.

❷ Meanwhile, cut each frankfurter sausage into 3 pieces. Thread the frankfurter pieces, courgette slices, corn cob slices, cherry tomatoes and baby onions alternately on to metal skewers. Brush with olive oil.

❸ Cook the skewers over hot coals, turning and brushing frequently with the oil, for 8–10 minutes. Meanwhile, brush the slices of baguette with oil and toast both sides on the barbecue. Unwrap the garlic bulbs and squeeze the cloves on to the bread. Season to taste with salt and pepper and drizzle over a little extra olive oil, if you like. Transfer the skewers to a large serving plate and serve immediately with the garlic toast.

Variation

Slice a baguette without cutting it right through. Spread with 2 crushed garlic cloves beaten into 115 g/4 oz butter. Wrap in foil and cook for 15 minutes.

Mustard & Honey Drumsticks

Chicken can taste rather bland, but this sweet-and-sour glaze gives it a wonderful piquancy and helps to keep it moist during cooking.

serves 4

8 chicken drumsticks

fresh parsley sprigs, to garnish

salad, to serve

Glaze

125 ml/4 fl oz clear honey

4 tbsp Dijon mustard

4 tbsp wholegrain mustard

4 tbsp white wine vinegar

2 tbsp sunflower oil

salt and pepper

Method

❶ Using a sharp knife, make 2–3 diagonal slashes in the chicken drumsticks and place them in a large, non-metallic dish.

❷ Mix all the ingredients for the glaze together in a jug and season to taste with salt and pepper. Pour the glaze over the drumsticks, turning until the drumsticks are well coated. Cover with clingfilm and leave to marinate in the refrigerator for at least 1 hour.

❸ Preheat the barbecue. Drain the chicken drumsticks, reserving the marinade. Cook the chicken over medium-hot coals, turning frequently and brushing with the reserved marinade, for 25–30 minutes, or until thoroughly cooked. Transfer to serving plates, garnish with fresh parsley sprigs and serve immediately with salad.

Variation

Try this glaze with pork spare ribs.
Marinate 900 g/2 lb spare ribs in the glaze for
1 hour. Cook over hot coals, turning frequently
and brushing with the glaze, for 15–20 minutes.

Sage & Lemon Poussins

Spatchcocked poussins are the ideal choice for a barbecue, as they are easy to handle and look attractive. You can buy them ready prepared or spatchcock them yourself.

serves 4

4 poussins, about 450 g/1 lb each

1 lemon

2 tbsp chopped fresh sage

salt and pepper

To garnish

fresh herb sprigs

lemon slices

Method

❶ Preheat the barbecue. To spatchcock the poussins, turn 1 bird breast-side down and, using strong kitchen scissors or poultry shears, cut through the skin and ribcage along both sides of the backbone, from tail to neck. Remove the backbone and turn the bird breast-side up. Press down firmly on the breastbone with the heel of your hand to flatten. Fold the wingtips underneath. Repeat with the remaining poussins.

❷ Thinly slice half the lemon and finely grate the rind of the other half. Mix the lemon rind and sage together in a small bowl. Loosen the skin over the breasts and legs of the poussins and insert the lemon and sage mixture. Tuck in the lemon slices and smooth the skin back firmly. Push a metal skewer into one wing, through the top of the breast and out of the other wing. Push a second skewer into one thigh, through the bottom of the breast and out of the other thigh. Season to taste with salt and pepper.

❸ Cook the poussins over medium-hot coals for 10–15 minutes on each side. Serve immediately, garnished with fresh herb sprigs and lemon slices.

Hot Red Chicken

Chicken pieces are used in this adaptation of a traditional Indian recipe for spring chickens, but you could substitute spatchcocked poussins if you prefer.

serves 4

1 tbsp curry paste

1 tbsp tomato ketchup

1 tsp Indian five-spice powder

1 fresh red chilli, deseeded and finely chopped

1 tsp Worcestershire sauce

1 tsp sugar

salt

8 skinless chicken pieces

vegetable oil, for brushing

naan bread, to serve

To garnish

lemon wedges

fresh coriander sprigs

Method

❶ Place the curry paste, tomato ketchup, five-spice powder, chilli, Worcestershire sauce and sugar in a small bowl, and stir until the sugar has dissolved. Season to taste with salt.

❷ Place the chicken pieces in a large, shallow, non-metallic dish and spoon the spice paste over them, rubbing it in well. Cover with clingfilm and leave to marinate in the refrigerator for up to 8 hours.

❸ Preheat the barbecue. Remove the chicken from the spice paste, discarding any remaining paste, and brush with oil. Cook the chicken over medium-hot coals, turning occasionally, for 25–30 minutes. Briefly heat the naan bread on the barbecue and serve with the chicken, garnished with lemon wedges and coriander sprigs.

Turkey Rolls

These herb-flavoured rolls conceal a soft centre of melted cheese as a lovely surprise. They are served here with redcurrant relish, but would also be delicious with a mild mustard sauce.

serves 4

2 tbsp sunflower oil

salt and pepper

4 tbsp chopped fresh marjoram

4 turkey breast steaks

4 tsp mild mustard

175 g/6 oz Emmenthal cheese, grated

1 leek, thinly sliced

Relish

115 g/4 oz redcurrants

2 tbsp chopped fresh mint

2 tsp clear honey

1 tsp red wine vinegar

Method

❶ Preheat the barbecue. To make the redcurrant relish, place all the ingredients in a bowl and mash well with a fork. Season to taste with salt and pepper. Cover with clingfilm and leave to chill in the refrigerator until required.

❷ Pour the oil into a small bowl, season to taste with pepper and stir in 2 teaspoons of the marjoram. Reserve. Place the turkey steaks between 2 sheets of clingfilm and beat with the side of a rolling pin to flatten. Season with salt and pepper and spread the mustard evenly over them. Divide the Emmenthal cheese, leek and remaining marjoram between the turkey steaks, roll up and tie securely with kitchen string.

❸ Brush the turkey rolls with the flavoured oil and cook over medium-hot coals, turning and brushing frequently with the remaining oil, for 30 minutes. Serve immediately with the relish.

Tarragon Turkey

This economical dish is quick and simple to prepare, and yet it tastes absolutely wonderful, not least because poultry and tarragon have a natural affinity.

serves 4

4 turkey breast steaks,
about 175 g/6 oz each
salt and pepper
4 tsp wholegrain mustard

8 fresh tarragon sprigs,
plus extra to garnish
4 smoked back bacon rashers
salad leaves, to serve

Method

❶ Preheat the barbecue. Season the turkey to taste with salt and pepper. Using a round-bladed knife, spread the mustard evenly over the turkey.

❷ Place 2 tarragon sprigs on top of each turkey breast and wrap a bacon rasher around to hold the herbs in place. Secure with a cocktail stick.

❸ Cook the turkey over medium-hot coals for 5–8 minutes on each side. Transfer to serving plates and garnish with tarragon sprigs. Serve with salad leaves.

Fruity Duck

Apricots and onions counteract the richness of the duck. Its high fat content makes it virtually self-basting, so it stays superbly moist. The duck looks particularly elegant garnished with spring onion tassels.

serves 4

4 duck breasts

115 g/4 oz ready-to-eat dried apricots

2 shallots, thinly sliced

2 tbsp clear honey

1 tsp sesame oil

2 tsp Chinese five-spice powder

4 spring onions, to garnish

Method

❶ Preheat the barbecue. Using a sharp knife, cut a long slit in the fleshy side of each duck breast to make a pocket. Divide the apricots and shallots between the pockets and secure with skewers.

❷ Mix the honey and sesame oil together in a small bowl and brush all over the duck. Sprinkle with the five-spice powder. To make the garnish, make a few cuts lengthways down the stem of each spring onion. Place in a bowl of ice-cold water and leave until the tassels open out. Drain well before using.

❸ Cook the duck over medium-hot coals for 6–8 minutes on each side. Remove the skewers, transfer to a large serving plate and garnish with the spring onion tassels. Serve immediately.

Variation

Substitute 4 pork chops for the duck and cook over medium-hot coals for 8–9 minutes on each side, or until thoroughly cooked.

Fish
& Seafood

Caribbean Fish Kebabs

Lightly spiced and marinated, these colourful kebabs look and taste delicious.
You can use any firm-textured fish, but for an authentic Caribbean flavour,
swordfish is perfect.

serves 6

1 kg/2 lb 4 oz swordfish steaks

3 tbsp olive oil

3 tbsp lime juice

1 garlic clove, finely chopped

1 tsp paprika

salt and pepper

3 onions, cut into wedges

6 tomatoes, cut into wedges

Method

❶ Using a sharp knife, cut the fish into 2.5-cm/1-inch cubes and place in a shallow, non-metallic dish. Place the oil, lime juice, garlic and paprika in a jug and mix well. Season to taste with salt and pepper. Pour the marinade over the fish, turning to coat evenly. Cover with clingfilm and leave to marinate in the refrigerator for 1 hour.

❷ Preheat the barbecue. Thread the fish cubes, onion wedges and tomato wedges alternately on to 6 long, presoaked wooden skewers. Reserve the marinade.

❸ Cook the kebabs over medium-hot coals for 8–10 minutes, turning and brushing frequently with the reserved marinade. When they are cooked through, transfer the kebabs to a large serving plate and serve immediately.

Variation

Instead of serving the kebabs with traditional baked potatoes, serve them with baked sweet potatoes.

Salmon with Mango Salsa

Although an oily fish, salmon can dry out easily on the fierce heat of the barbecue. Make sure that it is well coated with the citrus juice before you begin cooking.

serves 4

4 salmon steaks, about 175 g/6 oz each
finely grated rind and juice
of 1 lime or ½ lemon
salt and pepper

Salsa
1 large mango, peeled,
stoned and diced
1 red onion, finely chopped
2 passion fruit
2 fresh basil sprigs
2 tbsp lime juice
salt

Method

❶ Preheat the barbecue. Rinse the salmon steaks under cold running water, pat dry with kitchen paper and place in a large, shallow, non-metallic dish. Sprinkle with the lime rind and pour the juice over them. Season to taste with salt and pepper, cover and leave to stand while you make the salsa.

❷ Place the mango flesh in a bowl with the onion. Cut the passion fruit in half. Scoop out the seeds and the pulp with a teaspoon, and add them to the bowl. Tear the basil leaves and add them to the bowl with the lime juice. Season to taste with salt and stir well. Cover with clingfilm and reserve until required.

❸ Cook the salmon steaks over medium-hot coals for 3–4 minutes on each side. Serve immediately with the salsa.

Stuffed Sardines

Barbecued fresh sardines are always a popular choice. They are usually just plainly grilled, but here they are stuffed with herbs and coated in a mild spice mixture.

serves 6

15 g/½ oz fresh parsley, finely chopped

4 garlic cloves, finely chopped

12 fresh sardines, cleaned and scaled

3 tbsp lemon juice

85 g/3 oz plain flour

1 tsp ground cumin

salt and pepper

olive oil, for brushing

Method

❶ Place the parsley and garlic in a bowl and mix together. Rinse the fish inside and out under cold running water and pat dry with kitchen paper. Spoon the herb mixture into the fish cavities and pat the remainder all over the outside of the fish. Sprinkle the sardines with lemon juice and transfer to a large, shallow, non-metallic dish. Cover with clingfilm and leave to marinate in the refrigerator for 1 hour.

❷ Preheat the barbecue. Mix the flour and ground cumin together in a bowl, then season to taste with salt and pepper. Spread out the seasoned flour on a large plate and gently roll the sardines in the flour to coat.

❸ Brush the sardines with olive oil and cook over medium-hot coals for 3–4 minutes on each side. Serve immediately.

Orange & Lemon Peppered Monkfish

Although monkfish appears quite expensive, there is very little wastage as, apart from the central backbone, the entire tail is edible. Its flavour is meaty and succulent.

serves 6

2 oranges

2 lemons

2 monkfish tails, about 500 g/1 lb 2 oz
each, skinned and cut into 4 fillets

6 fresh lemon thyme sprigs

2 tbsp olive oil

salt

2 tbsp green peppercorns,
lightly crushed

To garnish

orange wedges

lemon wedges

Method

❶ Cut 8 orange slices and 8 lemon slices, reserving the remaining fruit. Rinse the monkfish fillets under cold running water and pat dry with kitchen paper. Place 1 fillet from each monkfish tail, cut side up, on a work surface and divide the citrus slices between them. Top with the lemon thyme. Reassemble the tails and tie them securely together at intervals with kitchen string or trussing thread. Place the tails in a large, shallow, non-metallic dish.

❷ Squeeze the juice from the remaining fruit and mix with the olive oil in a jug. Season to taste with salt, then spoon the mixture over the fish. Cover with clingfilm and leave to marinate in the refrigerator for up to 1 hour, spooning the marinade over the fish tails once or twice.

❸ Preheat the barbecue. Drain the monkfish tails, reserving the marinade. Sprinkle the crushed green peppercorns over the fish, pressing them in with your fingers. Cook the monkfish over medium-hot coals, turning and brushing frequently with the reserved marinade, for 20–25 minutes. Transfer to a chopping board, remove and discard the string and cut the monkfish tails into slices. Serve immediately, garnished with orange and lemon wedges.

Bacon-wrapped Trout

This classic, pan-fried combination is even more delicious cooked on the barbecue, as the smoky flavour of the bacon becomes more pronounced in contrast to the delicate flesh of the fish.

serves 4

4 trout, gutted	**To garnish**
4 smoked streaky bacon rashers, rinded	fresh parsley sprigs
4 tbsp plain flour	lemon wedges
salt and pepper	
2 tbsp olive oil	
2 tbsp lemon juice	
lamb's lettuce, to serve	

Method

❶ Preheat the barbecue. Rinse the trout inside and out under cold running water and pat dry with kitchen paper. Stretch the bacon using the back of a heavy, flat-bladed knife.

❷ Season the flour with salt and pepper and spread it out on a large, flat plate. Gently roll each trout in the seasoned flour until thoroughly coated. Beginning just below the head, wrap a rasher of bacon in a spiral along the length of each fish.

❸ Brush the trout with olive oil and cook over medium-hot coals for 5–8 minutes on each side. Transfer to 4 large serving plates and drizzle with the lemon juice. Garnish with parsley and lemon wedges and serve with lamb's lettuce.

Sizzling Scallops

This is a new and great way to cook scallops on the barbecue. You can also use other shellfish, such as oysters, if you prefer.

serves 4

1 lemon

6 tbsp olive oil

salt and pepper

12 prepared scallops

115 g/4 oz fresh wholemeal breadcrumbs

55 g/2 oz butter, melted

lemon wedges, to garnish (optional)

Method

❶ Finely grate the lemon rind, then place it in a dish with the olive oil and mix together. Season to taste. Add the scallops, tossing to coat, then cover and leave to marinate for 30 minutes.

❷ Preheat the barbecue. Place the breadcrumbs in a large bowl. Add the scallops, one at a time, and toss until they are well coated, then thread on to individual presoaked wooden skewers. Drizzle with the melted butter.

❸ Cook the breaded scallops over medium-hot coals, turning once, for 8–10 minutes. Transfer to a large serving dish, garnish with lemon wedges, if you like, and serve immediately.

Chargrilled Devils

This is a barbecue version of the classic appetizer 'angels on horseback', and goes to prove how sophisticated and elegant alfresco dining can be.

serves 4

36 fresh oysters
18 streaky bacon rashers, rinded
1 tbsp mild paprika
1 tsp cayenne pepper

Sauce
1 fresh red chilli, deseeded and finely chopped
1 garlic clove, finely chopped
1 shallot, finely chopped
2 tbsp finely chopped fresh parsley
2 tbsp lemon juice
salt and pepper

Method

❶ Preheat the barbecue. Open the oysters, catching the juice from the shells in a bowl. Cut the oysters from the bottom shells, reserve and tip any remaining juice into the bowl. To make the sauce, add the red chilli, garlic, shallot, parsley and lemon juice to the bowl, then season to taste with salt and pepper and mix well. Cover the bowl with clingfilm and leave to chill in the refrigerator until required.

❷ Cut each bacon rasher in half across the centre. Season the oysters with paprika and cayenne, then roll each one up in half a bacon rasher. Spear each wrapped oyster with a presoaked cocktail stick or thread 9 on to each of 4 presoaked wooden skewers.

❸ Cook over hot coals, turning frequently, for 5 minutes, or until the bacon is well browned and crispy. Transfer to a large serving plate and serve immediately with the sauce.

Variation

You can replace the shallot with a small, finely chopped onion and the fresh parsley with the same amount of snipped fresh chives, if you prefer.

Spanish Prawns

**These fresh prawns are served with a fiery tomato and chilli sauce.
If you prefer a milder flavour, you can reduce the number of chillies.**

serves 6

1 bunch of fresh flat-leaved parsley

36 large, raw Mediterranean prawns,
peeled, with tails left on, and deveined

3–4 tbsp olive oil

lemon wedges, to garnish

Sauce

6 fresh red chillies

1 onion, chopped

2 garlic cloves, chopped

500 g/1 lb 2 oz tomatoes, chopped

3 tbsp olive oil

pinch of sugar

salt and pepper

Method

❶ Preheat the barbecue. Chop enough parsley to fill 2 tablespoons and reserve. To make the sauce, deseed and chop the chillies, then put into a food processor with the onion and garlic and process until finely chopped. Add the tomatoes and olive oil and process to a purée.

❷ Transfer the mixture to a saucepan set over a very low heat, stir in the sugar and season to taste with salt and pepper. Simmer very gently, without boiling, for 15 minutes. Transfer the sauce to an earthenware bowl and place on the side of the barbecue to keep warm.

❸ Rinse the prawns under cold running water and pat dry on kitchen paper. Mix the parsley and olive oil in a dish, add the prawns and toss well to coat. Cook the prawns over medium-hot coals for 3 minutes on each side, or until they have changed colour. Transfer to a plate, garnish with lemon wedges and serve with the sauce.

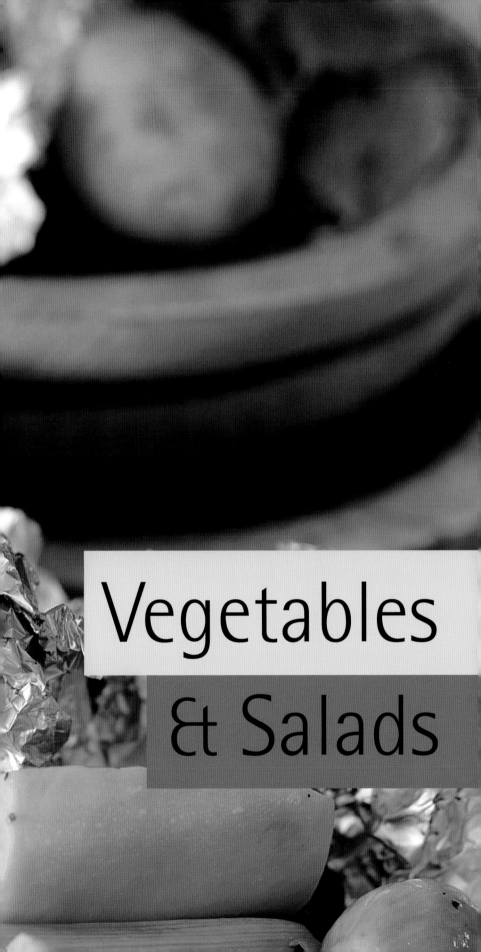

Vegetables
& Salads

Stuffed Tomato Parcels

An unusual filling for stuffed tomatoes, the spinach and cheese are given extra flavour with toasted sunflower seeds.

serves 4

1 tbsp olive oil	pinch of freshly grated nutmeg
2 tbsp sunflower seeds	salt and pepper
1 onion, finely chopped	4 beef tomatoes
1 garlic clove, finely chopped	140 g/5 oz mozzarella cheese, diced
500 g/1 lb 2 oz fresh spinach, thick stalks removed and leaves shredded	

Method

❶ Preheat the barbecue. Heat the oil in a heavy-based saucepan. Add the sunflower seeds and cook, stirring constantly, for 2 minutes, or until golden. Add the onion and cook over a low heat, stirring occasionally, for 5 minutes, or until softened but not browned. Add the garlic and spinach, cover and cook for 2–3 minutes, or until the spinach has wilted. Remove the saucepan from the heat and season to taste with nutmeg, salt and pepper. Leave to cool.

❷ Using a sharp knife, cut off and reserve a thin slice from the top of each tomato and scoop out the flesh with a teaspoon, taking care not to pierce the shell. Chop the flesh and stir it into the spinach mixture with the mozzarella cheese.

❸ Fill the tomato shells with the spinach and cheese mixture and replace the tops. Cut 4 squares of foil, each large enough to enclose a tomato. Place one tomato in the centre of each square and fold up the sides to enclose securely. Cook over hot coals, turning occasionally, for 10 minutes. Serve immediately in the parcels.

Potato Fans

These garlic-flavoured roast potatoes make a wonderful alternative to baked potatoes. Allow plenty of time for cooking.

serves 6

6 large potatoes, scrubbed but not peeled

2 tbsp garlic-flavoured olive oil

Method

❶ Preheat the barbecue. Using a sharp knife, make a series of cuts across the potatoes almost all the way through. Cut out 6 squares of foil, each large enough to enclose a potato.

❷ Place a potato on each square of foil and brush generously with the garlic-flavoured oil. Fold up the sides of the foil to enclose the potatoes completely.

❸ Cook over hot coals, turning occasionally, for 1 hour. To serve, open the foil parcels and gently pinch the potatoes to open up the fans.

Courgette & Cheese Parcels

These delicately flavoured, melt-in-the-mouth stuffed courgettes are ideal if you are serving food to both meat-eaters and vegetarians, as the parcels can be cooked in the barbecue embers and so avoid any contact with meat on the grill.

serves 8

1 small bunch of fresh mint

8 courgettes

1 tbsp olive oil, plus extra for brushing

115 g/4 oz feta cheese,
cut into strips

pepper

Method

❶ Preheat the barbecue. Using a sharp knife, finely chop enough mint to fill 1 tablespoon. Reserve until required. Cut out 8 rectangles of foil, each large enough to enclose a courgette, and brush lightly with olive oil. Cut a slit along the length of each courgette and place them on the foil rectangles.

❷ Insert strips of feta cheese along the slits in the courgettes, then drizzle the olive oil over the top, sprinkle with the reserved chopped mint and season to taste with pepper. Fold in the sides of the foil and seal the edges securely to enclose the cheese-stuffed courgettes completely.

❸ Bake the courgette parcels in the barbecue embers for 30 minutes. Carefully unwrap the parcels and serve immediately.

Variation

If you like, substitute mozzarella cheese or fontina cheese for the feta cheese and replace the mint with the same amount of fresh parsley.

Vegetarian Brochettes

The great thing about tofu – apart from the fact that it is packed
with protein – is its ability to absorb other flavours, in this case
a mustard and honey flavoured glaze.

serves 4

2 courgettes

1 yellow pepper, deseeded
and quartered

225 g/8 oz firm tofu (drained weight)

4 cherry tomatoes

4 baby onions

8 button mushrooms

Honey glaze

2 tbsp olive oil

1 tbsp Meaux mustard

1 tbsp clear honey

salt and pepper

Method

❶ Preheat the barbecue. Using a
vegetable peeler, peel off strips of skin
along the length of the courgettes to
leave alternate yellow and green stripes,
then cut each courgette into 8 thick slices.
Cut each of the yellow pepper quarters in
half. Cut the drained tofu into
2.5-cm/1-inch cubes.

❷ Thread the pieces of pepper, courgette
slices, tofu cubes, cherry tomatoes, baby
onions and button mushrooms on to
4 metal skewers. To make the glaze, mix
the olive oil, mustard and honey together
in a jug and season to taste with salt
and pepper.

❸ Brush the brochettes with the honey
glaze and cook over medium-hot coals,
turning and brushing frequently with the
glaze, for 8–10 minutes. Serve.

Variation

*You can also make vegetable brochettes. Omit the
tofu and use aubergine chunks, courgette chunks
and small strips of red pepper.*

Summer Vegetable Parcels

You can use any baby vegetables you like – patty pan squash, corn cobs and plum tomatoes look attractive and add colour. Serve with grilled meat or fish for a substantial barbecue main course.

serves 4

1 kg/2 lb 4 oz mixed baby vegetables, such as carrots, patty pan squash, corn cobs, plum tomatoes, leeks, courgettes and onions
1 lemon

115 g/4 oz unsalted butter
3 tbsp chopped mixed fresh herbs, such as parsley, thyme and chervil
2 garlic cloves
salt and pepper

Method

❶ Preheat the barbecue. Cut out 4 x 30-cm/12-inch squares of foil and divide the vegetables equally between them.

❷ Using a grater, finely grate the lemon rind, then squeeze the juice from the lemon and reserve until required. Put the lemon rind, butter, herbs and garlic into a food processor and process until blended, then season to taste with salt and pepper. Alternatively, beat together in a bowl until blended.

❸ Divide the flavoured butter equally between the vegetables, dotting it on top. Fold up the sides of the foil to enclose the vegetables, sealing securely. Cook over medium-hot coals, turning occasionally, for 25–30 minutes. Open the parcels, sprinkle with the reserved lemon juice and serve immediately.

Variation

If baby vegetables are unavailable, then use larger vegetables cut into small pieces, such as courgette and carrot batons and aubergine chunks.

Corn-on-the-Cob with Blue Cheese Dressing

Corn cobs are delicious grilled on the barbecue. Cook them as soon after purchase as possible because they quickly lose their sweetness as their natural sugars convert to starch.

serves 6

140 g/5 oz Danish Blue cheese

140 g/5 oz curd cheese

125 ml/4 fl oz natural Greek yogurt

salt and pepper

6 corn cobs in their husks

Method

❶ Preheat the barbecue. Crumble the Danish Blue cheese, then place in a bowl. Beat with a wooden spoon until creamy. Beat in the curd cheese until thoroughly blended. Gradually beat in the yogurt and season to taste with salt and pepper. Cover with clingfilm and leave to chill in the refrigerator until required.

❷ Fold back the husks on each corn cob and remove the silks. Smooth the husks back into place. Cut out 6 rectangles of foil, each large enough to enclose a corn cob. Wrap the corn cobs in the foil.

❸ Cook the corn cobs over hot coals, turning frequently, for 15–20 minutes. Unwrap the corn cobs and discard the foil. Peel back the husk on one side of each and trim off with a sharp knife or kitchen scissors. Serve immediately with the blue cheese dressing.

Cajun Vegetables

These spicy vegetables would be a perfect accompaniment to some colourful Caribbean Fish Kebabs (see page 44).

serves 4

4 corn cobs
2 sweet potatoes, scrubbed but not peeled
25 g/1 oz butter, melted

Spice mix
2 tsp paprika
1 tsp ground cumin
1 tsp ground coriander
1 tsp ground black pepper
½–1 tsp chilli powder

Method

❶ Preheat the barbecue. To make the spice mix, mix all the ingredients together in a small bowl.

❷ Remove the husks and silks from the corn cobs, then cut each cob into 4 equal chunks. Cut the sweet potatoes into thick slices, but do not peel. Brush the corn chunks and sweet potato slices with melted butter and sprinkle with some spice mix.

❸ Cook the corn cobs and sweet potatoes over medium-hot coals, turning frequently, for 12–15 minutes. Brush with more melted butter and sprinkle with extra spice mixture during cooking. Transfer the corn and sweet potatoes to a large serving plate and serve immediately.

Prune, Apricot & Onion Skewers

These flavoursome, fruity skewers would go well with plain grilled pork chops, duck breasts, lamb steaks or kebabs, as their sweetness would counteract the richness of the meat.

serves 4

500 g/1 lb 2 oz baby onions

175 g/6 oz prunes, stoned

225 g/8 oz dried apricots, stoned

5-cm/2-inch cinnamon stick

225 ml/8 fl oz white wine

2 tbsp chilli sauce

2 tbsp sunflower oil

Method

❶ Cut the tops off the onions and peel off the skin. Reserve until required. Place the prunes, apricots, cinnamon and wine in a heavy-based saucepan and bring to the boil. Reduce the heat and simmer for 5 minutes. Drain, reserving the cooking liquid, and leave the fruit until cool enough to handle.

❷ Return the cooking liquid and cinnamon stick to the saucepan, return to the boil and boil until reduced by half. Remove the saucepan from the heat and remove and discard the cinnamon stick. Stir in the chilli sauce and oil.

❸ Thread the prunes, apricots and onions on to several metal skewers. Cook over medium-hot coals, turning and brushing frequently with the wine mixture, for 10 minutes. Serve immediately.

Aubergines with Tsatziki

This makes a delicious appetizer for a barbecue party or can be served as part of a vegetarian barbecue meze with Stuffed Tomato Parcels (see page 62), or Courgette & Cheese Parcels (see page 66).

serves 4

2 tbsp olive oil	**Tsatziki**
salt and pepper	½ cucumber
2 aubergines, thinly sliced	200 ml/7 fl oz natural Greek yogurt
	4 spring onions, finely chopped
	1 garlic clove, finely chopped
	3 tbsp chopped fresh mint
	salt and pepper
	1 fresh mint sprig, to garnish

Method

❶ Preheat the barbecue. To make the tsatziki, finely chop the cucumber. Place the yogurt in a bowl and beat well until smooth. Stir in the cucumber, spring onions, garlic and mint until distributed evenly through the yogurt. Season to taste with salt and pepper. Transfer to a serving bowl, cover with clingfilm and leave to chill in the refrigerator until required.

❷ Season the olive oil with salt and pepper, then brush the aubergine slices with the oil.

❸ Cook the aubergines over hot coals for 5 minutes on each side, brushing with more oil, if necessary. Transfer to a large serving plate and serve immediately with the tsatziki, garnished with a mint sprig.

Tropical Rice Salad

Rice salads are always popular and this colourful, fruity mixture goes especially well with barbecued meat or chicken.

serves 4

115 g/4 oz long-grain rice	**Dressing**
salt and pepper	1 tbsp groundnut oil
4 spring onions	1 tbsp hazelnut oil
225 g/8 oz canned pineapple pieces in	1 tbsp light soy sauce
natural juice	1 garlic clove, finely chopped
200 g/7 oz canned sweetcorn, drained	1 tsp chopped fresh root ginger
2 red peppers, deseeded and diced	
3 tbsp sultanas	

Method

❶ Cook the rice in a large saucepan of lightly salted boiling water for 15 minutes, or until tender. Drain thoroughly and rinse under cold running water. Place the rice in a large serving bowl.

❷ Using a sharp knife, finely chop the spring onions. Drain the pineapple pieces, reserving the juice in a jug. Add the pineapple pieces, sweetcorn, red peppers, chopped spring onions and sultanas to the rice and mix lightly.

❸ Add all the dressing ingredients to the reserved pineapple juice, whisking well, and season to taste with salt and pepper. Pour the dressing over the salad and toss until the salad is thoroughly coated. Serve immediately.

Variation

Try other flavoured nut oils, such as walnut oil or sesame oil. You can also substitute sunflower oil for the groundnut oil, if you like.

Tabbouleh

This Middle Eastern salad is increasingly fashionable. It is a classic accompaniment for lamb, but goes well with most grilled meat.

serves 4

175 g/6 oz bulgar wheat

3 tbsp extra virgin olive oil

4 tbsp lemon juice

salt and pepper

4 spring onions

1 green pepper, deseeded and sliced

4 tomatoes, chopped

2 tbsp chopped fresh parsley

2 tbsp chopped fresh mint

8 black olives, stoned

fresh mint sprigs, to garnish

Method

❶ Place the bulgar wheat in a large bowl and add enough cold water to cover. Leave to stand for 30 minutes, or until the wheat has doubled in size. Drain well and press out as much liquid as possible. Spread out the wheat on kitchen paper to dry.

❷ Place the wheat in a serving bowl. Mix the olive oil and lemon juice together in a jug and season to taste with salt and pepper. Pour the lemon mixture over the wheat and leave to marinate for 1 hour.

❸ Using a sharp knife, finely chop the spring onions, then add to the salad with the green pepper, tomatoes, parsley and mint and toss lightly to mix. Top the salad with the olives and garnish with fresh mint sprigs, then serve.

Variation

Use different types of fresh tomatoes – try vine-ripened tomatoes, which have a delicate, sweet flavour, or cherry tomatoes, cut in half.

Cheese & Walnut Pasta Salad

This is an ideal salad to serve with a barbecue, as it is not just a pasta salad, which can seem a little mundane, but also includes a colourful mix of crisp salad leaves.

serves 4

225 g/8 oz dried fusilli

salt and pepper

225 g/8 oz dolcelatte cheese

100 g/3½ oz mixed salad leaves, such as oakleaf lettuce, radina, baby spinach, rocket and lamb's lettuce

115 g/4 oz walnut halves

4 tbsp sunflower oil

2 tbsp walnut oil

2 tbsp red wine vinegar

Method

❶ Cook the pasta in a large saucepan of lightly salted boiling water for 8–10 minutes, or until tender, but still firm to the bite. Drain, rinse under cold running water and drain again.

❷ Using a sharp knife, cut the dolcelatte cheese into cubes. Place the salad leaves in a large serving bowl and add the cooked pasta. Sprinkle the dolcelatte cheese on top.

❸ Preheat the grill to medium. Place the walnut halves on a large baking tray and cook under the grill for a few minutes, or until lightly toasted. Leave to cool. Mix the sunflower oil, walnut oil and red wine vinegar together in a jug and season to taste with salt and pepper. Pour the dressing over the salad, toss lightly, then top with the toasted walnuts.

Red & Green Salad

Beetroot and orange is a classic combination and here they are mixed with tender baby spinach leaves to make a dramatic and colourful warm salad.

serves 4

650 g/1 lb 7 oz cooked beetroot, peeled

3 tbsp extra virgin olive oil

juice of 1 orange

1 tsp caster sugar

1 tsp fennel seeds

salt and pepper

115 g/4 oz fresh baby spinach leaves

Method

❶ Using a sharp knife, dice the cooked beetroot and reserve until required. Heat the olive oil in a small, heavy-based saucepan. Add the orange juice, sugar and fennel seeds and season to taste with salt and pepper. Stir constantly until the sugar has dissolved.

❷ Add the reserved beetroot to the saucepan and stir gently to coat. Remove the saucepan from the heat.

❸ Arrange the baby spinach leaves in a large salad bowl. Spoon the warmed beetroot on top and serve immediately.

Desserts

Mixed Fruit Kebabs

You can use almost any firm-fleshed fruit to make these colourful,
quick and easy kebabs. Remember to soak the wooden skewers in cold water
before using to prevent burning.

serves 4

2 nectarines, halved and stoned	2 bananas, peeled and thickly sliced
2 kiwi fruit	8 strawberries, hulled
4 red plums	1 tbsp clear honey
1 mango, peeled, halved and stoned	3 tbsp Cointreau

Method

❶ Cut the nectarine halves in half again and place in a large, shallow dish. Peel and quarter the kiwi fruit. Cut the plums in half and remove the stones. Cut the mango flesh into chunks and add to the dish with the kiwi fruit, plums, bananas and strawberries.

❷ Mix the honey and Cointreau together in a jug until well blended. Pour the mixture over the fruit and toss lightly to coat. Cover with clingfilm and leave to marinate in the refrigerator for 1 hour.

❸ Preheat the barbecue. Drain the fruit, reserving the marinade. Thread the fruit on to several presoaked wooden skewers and cook over medium-hot coals, turning and brushing frequently with the reserved marinade, for 5–7 minutes, then serve.

Barbecued Baked Apples

**When they are wrapped in kitchen foil, apples bake to perfection
on the barbecue and make a delightful finale to any meal.**

serves 4

4 medium cooking apples

25 g/1 oz walnuts, chopped

25 g/1 oz ground almonds

25 g/1 oz light muscovado sugar

25 g/1 oz cherries, chopped

25 g/1 oz stem ginger, chopped

1 tbsp Amaretto (optional)

50 g/1¾ oz butter

whipping cream or natural yogurt,
to serve

Method

❶ Core the apples and, using a sharp knife, score each one around the middle to prevent the skins from splitting while cooking on the barbecue.

❷ To make the filling, mix together the walnuts, almonds, sugar, cherries, ginger and Amaretto, if using, in a small bowl.

❸ Spoon some filling mixture into each apple, pushing it down into the hollowed-out core. Mound a little of the filling mixture on top of each apple.

❹ Place each apple on a large square of double thickness foil and generously dot all over with the butter. Gather up and seal the foil so that the apple is completely enclosed.

❺ Barbecue the foil parcels containing the apples over hot coals for 25–30 minutes or until tender.

❻ Transfer the apples to warm, individual serving plates. Serve with lashings of whipped cream or thick natural yogurt.

Variation

If the coals are dying down, place the kitchen foil parcels directly on to the coals, raking them up around the apples. Barbecue for 25–30 minutes and serve with whipped cream or natural yogurt.

Banana Sizzles

Bananas are particularly sweet and delicious when grilled –
and conveniently come with their own protective wrapping.

serves 4

3 tbsp butter, softened	pinch of ground cinnamon
2 tbsp dark rum	4 bananas
1 tbsp orange juice	orange zest, to decorate
4 tbsp dark muscovado sugar	

Method

❶ Preheat the barbecue. Beat the butter with the rum, orange juice, sugar and cinnamon in a small bowl until thoroughly blended and smooth.

❷ Place the bananas, without peeling, over hot coals and cook, turning frequently, for 6–8 minutes, or until the skins are blackened.

❸ Transfer the bananas to serving plates, slit the skins and cut partially through the flesh lengthways. Divide the flavoured butter between the bananas, decorate with orange zest and serve.

Recipe List

- Aubergines with Tsatziki *78* • Bacon Koftas *26* • Bacon-wrapped Trout *52*

- Banana Sizzles *94* • Barbecued Baked Apples *92* • Best Ever Burgers *12*

- Cajun Vegetables *74* • Caribbean Fish Kebabs *44* • Chargrilled Devils *56*

- Cheese & Walnut Pasta Salad *84* • Corn-on-the-Cob with Blue Cheese Dressing *72*

- Courgette & Cheese Parcels *66* • Fabulous Frankfurter Skewers *28* • Fruity Duck *40*

- Hot Red Chicken *34* • Luxury Cheeseburgers *14* • Meatballs on Sticks *24*

- Minted Lamb Steaks *18* • Mixed Fruit Kebabs *90* • Mustard & Honey Drumsticks *30*

- Normandy Brochettes *20* • Orange & Lemon Peppered Monkfish *50*

- Potato Fans *64* • Prune, Apricot & Onion Skewers *76* • Rack & Ruin *16*

- Red & Green Salad *86* • Sage & Lemon Poussins *32* • Salmon with Mango Salsa *46*

- Sausages with Barbecue Sauce *22* • Sizzling Scallops *54* • Spanish Prawns *58*

- Stuffed Sardines *48* • Stuffed Tomato Parcels *62* • Summer Vegetable Parcels *70*

- Tabasco Steaks with Watercress Butter *10* • Tabbouleh *82* • Tarragon Turkey *38*

- Tropical Rice Salad *80* • Turkey Rolls *36* • Vegetarian Brochettes *68*